JOKES
AND RIDDLES

By the editors of OWL Magazine

OWL

Greey de Pencier Books

© 1987, Greey de Pencier Books Inc.; originally published as OWL Jokes and Riddles, © 1983. No part of this book may be reproduced or copied in any form without written permission from the publisher.

ISBN 0-919872-85-9

OWL and the OWL character are trademarks of Owl Communications.
Books from OWL are published in Canada by Greey de Pencier Books Inc., 179 John St., Suite 500, Toronto, Ontario M5T 3G5.

Published simultaneously in the United States in 1992 by Firefly Books (U.S.) Inc., P.O. Box 1338, Ellicott Station, Buffalo, NY 1420?

Canadian Cataloguing in Publication Data
Main entry under title:
Jokes and Riddles

First published, 1983, under title
Owl's Jokes and Riddles.
ISBN 0-919872-85-9

1. Animals - Anecdotes, facetiae, satire, etc.
2. Wit and Humor, Juvenile. I. Dingwall, Laima, 1953 - . II. Weissman, Joe, 1947 -. III. Title: Owl's jokes and riddles.

PZ8.7.J64 1987   j828'.91402   C87-093422-8

Edited by Laima Dingwall
Cartoons by Joe Weissmann
Cover design by Wycliffe Smith
Cover illustration by Vesna Krstanovich

F G H

Printed in Canada

Q. What kind of ears do mountains have?

A. Mountaineers.

Q. What do you call a seagull that flies over the bay?

A. A bagel.

Q. How did the firefly feel when it ran into the fan?

A. De-lighted.

Q. Where does a lamb go for a haircut?

A. To the ba-ba shop.

Q. What is as big as a hippo but weighs nothing?

A. A hippo's shadow.

Introduction

Q. Why did the people at OWL Magazine write a joke book?

A. We thought it'd be a hoot.

Sorry, that was the best *we* could do on that subject—but we promise that the hundreds of jokes and riddles that follow on the next pages are much better.

Since we began OWL magazine in 1976, thousands of readers have sent in jokes. Before our mailbags burst, we thought we'd gather our favorites together in a book, along with some real things that are very funny. Whenever you laugh, please give a nod of thanks to all the OWL readers who helped make this book possible.

Whatsit?

If you can't believe your eyes, turn to page 94 to see what's happening here.

7

The Deep Daffy Sea

Q. What do you get when you cross a fish with an elephant?
A. Swimming trunks.

Q. What did the Cinderella fish wear to the ball?
A. Glass flippers.

Q. What fish are the richest?
A. Goldfish.

Q. What do you get when you cross an octopus with a hen?
A. A chicken with drumsticks for everyone.

Q. What do you call a frightened skindiver?

A. Chicken of the sea.

Q. What sits on the bottom of the ocean and shakes?

A. A nervous wreck.

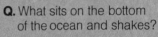

Q. What animals are weight watchers?

A. Fish, because they carry their scales with them at all times.

9

Q. What did the boy octopus say to the girl octopus?

A. I want to hold your hand hand hand hand hand hand hand hand.

Q. What goes clomp, clomp, clomp, clomp, clomp, clomp, clomp, squoosh?

A. An octopus with one shoe off.

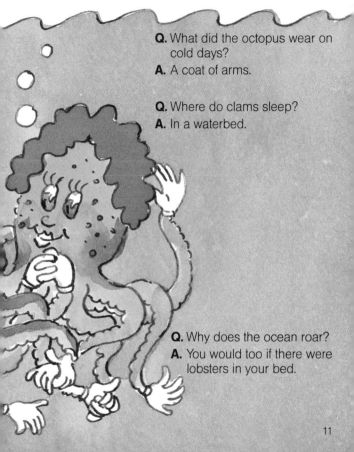

Q. What did the octopus wear on cold days?
A. A coat of arms.

Q. Where do clams sleep?
A. In a waterbed.

Q. Why does the ocean roar?
A. You would too if there were lobsters in your bed.

11

Q. Why are fish so smart?
A. Because they travel in schools.

Q. How do you know that the ocean is friendly?
A. Because it waves.

Q. How do you stop fish from smelling?
A. Cut off their noses.

Q. Why is the ocean salty?
A. Because fish don't like pepper.

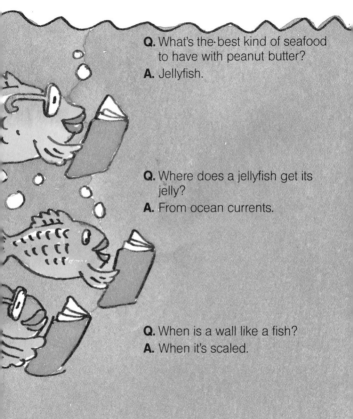

Q. What's the best kind of seafood to have with peanut butter?
A. Jellyfish.

Q. Where does a jellyfish get its jelly?
A. From ocean currents.

Q. When is a wall like a fish?
A. When it's scaled.

13

Terrific Twisters

We hope that you never see or hear seven silly squids singing sentimental songs. But if you repeat that twister and the others on these pages five times, as fast as you can, you might feel as if squids are sliding up and down your tongue.

Little lemmings love lemon liniment.

Would a wooly woodpecker whisper?

Cheep, cheep chirped the chirpy chickadee.

The boar's brass band bored the boring bear.

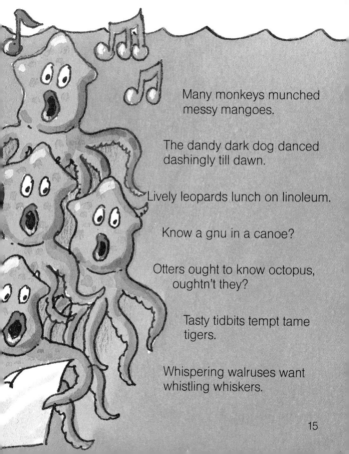

Many monkeys munched messy mangoes.

The dandy dark dog danced dashingly till dawn.

Lively leopards lunch on linoleum.

Know a gnu in a canoe?

Otters ought to know octopus, oughtn't they?

Tasty tidbits tempt tame tigers.

Whispering walruses want whistling whiskers.

15

Whatsit?

Turn to page 94 for some ducky facts about this picture.

Puttering Around the Pond

Q. Why does a frog have such an easy life?

A. Because it eats whatever bugs it.

Q. What does a frog say when it washes car windows?

A. Rub it, rub it, rub it.

Q. Why do bumblebees hum?

A. Because they don't know the words.

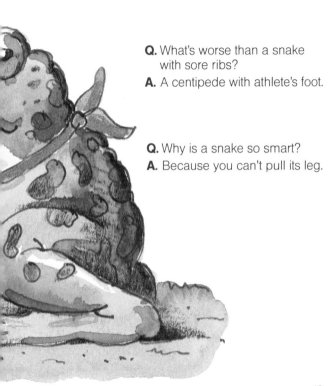

Q. What's worse than a snake with sore ribs?

A. A centipede with athlete's foot.

Q. Why is a snake so smart?

A. Because you can't pull its leg.

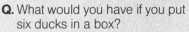

Q. What would you have if you put six ducks in a box?
A. A box of quackers.

Q. What's smarter than a talking horse?
A. A spelling bee.

Q. What do you call two spiders that were just married?
A. Newly webs.

Q. Why did the grasshopper go to the doctor?
A. Because he felt jumpy.

RITZY

Q. How did the firefly feel when he ran into the fan?
A. De-lighted.

Q What kind of suit does a duck wear?
A. A duck-sedo

Q. What happens to ducks when they fly upside-down?
A. They quack up.

21

Whatsit?

Is this feathered athlete for real? Find out on page 94.

Down on the Funny Farm

Q. What do you get when you cross a chicken with a bell?

A. An alarm cluck.

Q. What do you get when you cross a dog with a chicken?

A. Pooched eggs.

Q. Why are chickens often shooed out of the yard?

A. Because they use fowl language.

Q. Why did the chicken cross the road?

A. To get to the other side.

Q. Why did the chicken cross the playground?

A. To get to the other slide.

Q. Why does a chicken lay one egg at a time?

A. Because one egg is "un oeuf."

25

Q. Where does a lamb go for a haircut?
A. To the ba-ba shop.

Q. What do you call a pig's laundry?
A. Hog wash!

Q. What do you do for a sore pig?
A. Put on some oinkment.

Q. What do you call a cow that's eating grass?
A. A lawn moo-er.

Q. What's the most important use for cowhide?
A. It keeps the cow together.

Q. How do you get a cow excited?
A. Take it to the moo-vies!

Q. What do you call a bull when he is sleeping?
A. A bulldozer.

Q. If pigs wear wigs, what do piglets wear?
A. Wiglets.

Q. Why did the farmer take a milk bath?
A. He couldn't find a cow tall enough for a shower.

Q. What do you use to paint a rabbit?
A. Hare spray.

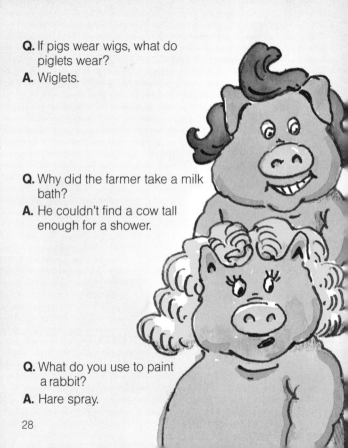

Q. Why do cows wear bells?
A. Because their horns don't work.

Q. What did the colt say when he coughed?
A. Excuse me, I'm a little horse.

Q. Why are goats hard to talk to?
A. Because they always butt in.

Q. What do you call a cow wearing a crown?

A. A dairy queen.

Q. What do you get when you cross a car with a cow?

A. An automoobile.

Q. Why can't you tell secrets on a farm?

A. Because the corn has ears, the potatoes have eyes, the grass whispers and the horses carry tails.

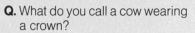

Q. What did the baby corn say to the mother corn?

A. I want pop corn.

Q. What animals took the least amount of baggage onto Noah's Ark?

A. The fox and the rooster. All they had between them was a brush and a comb.

Q. What do you get when you cross an owl with a goat?

A. A hootenanny.

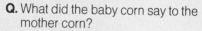

Whatsit?

Did you ever see a sheep trotting? Find out more on page 94.

EUREKA!

If you ever had a bright idea but were afraid everyone would laugh, take heart. What follows are some real inventions that at first seem silly, but once you think about them, they're quite good ideas after all.

The people at Vancouver Aquarium in British Columbia, Canada, are always looking for ways to save energy. Instead of plugging their string of 50 Christmas tree lights into a wall socket, they plug it into two electric eels. What a bright idea!

As sheep get older their teeth become weak and break. When this happens they have trouble eating and often die sooner than they should. So a dentist in Edinburgh, Scotland, designed a set of false sheep teeth. They're being tested now. Baa, baa. Clack, clack.

Every time the people of Göppingen, West Germany, take a drink of water, they thank six special goldfish. These goldfish—which come from the Nile River in Egypt—live in an aquarium fed by the city's tap water. In clean water they give off more than 1,000 very tiny electric shocks each second. If they stopped sending out shocks, it'd be a sign that the water may be unfit to drink. Here's to fish power!

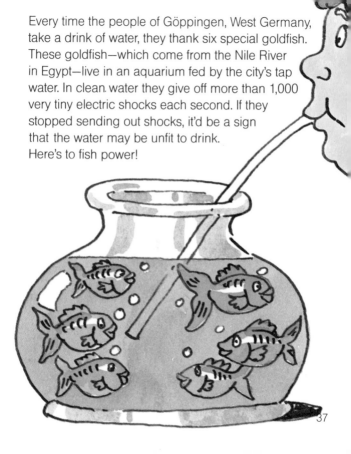

Among birds, rails are notoriously poor fliers and, unfortunately, when they walk they don't always look both ways before crossing a street. To help, the people of Newport Bay, near Los Angeles, California, U.S.A., installed special bird crosswalks. Now whenever a driver there comes to a "railway crossing," the rails have the right of way.

Pigeons strapped to the belly of a helicopter? It's not odd when they are trained in sea rescue. Because pigeons have keen eyesight, they can see brightly colored rafts, life jackets or flares about 30 seconds before people can. The idea is that when the pigeons spot something they peck a switch on the outside of the copter to alert the pilot.

Whatsit?

Don't give this invention the boot—it's an amazing feat of imagination. See page 94 for details.

Human Humor

Q. A family wanted to catch some mice but couldn't find any cheese for the mousetrap. So they cut out a picture of some cheese and put this in instead. What do you think they found in the trap in the morning?

A. A picture of a mouse.

Q. Why did the little girl take hay to bed?

A. To feed her nightmare.

Q. Why did no one play cards on Noah's Ark?

A. Because Noah always sat on the deck.

Q. Why does Santa enjoy gardening so much?

A. Because he loves to ho, ho, ho.

CLACK!

Q. Why did the boy put ice in his father's bed?

A. So he could have a cold pop.

Q. Why does a golfer wear two pairs of pants?

A. In case he or she makes a hole in one.

Q. Why are baseball players so rich?

A. Because they play on diamonds.

Q. Why are movie stars such cool people?

A. They have many fans.

Q. Why do carpenters believe there is no such thing as stone?

A. Because they never saw it.

Whatsit?

Is this a policeman facing up to his responsibilities?
See page 94 for news.

Going to Pieces

Q. What nail does a carpenter hate to hit with a hammer?

A. A thumbnail.

Q. When do broken bones make themselves useful?

A. When they begin to knit.

Q. What two animals always go with you?

A. Your calves.

Q. If a kid loses a knee, where does he or she go to get a new one?

A. To a butcher shop where kid knees are sold.

OUCH!

Body Tricks

Fool your friends by getting their bodies to play tricks on them. Start off by challenging a friend to lift your hand off your head. Turn the page to find out how this and five other body tricks work.

To set up the trick on the previous page, drape your hand over the top of your head and keep your forearm horizontal. Then tell your friend to try to pick up your arm. It'll be impossible because your friend will be trying to lift up your entire body—not just your hand.

Heavy Heads

You can trick several people at once into believing that you have "glued" their heads to the wall.

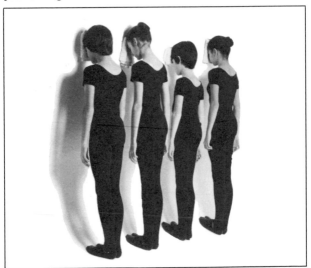

Tell your friends to keep their hands to their sides and face the wall so their foreheads and toes touch it, then give them these instructions:

1. Move your right foot directly behind your left.

2. Move your left foot directly behind your right.

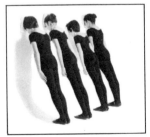

3. Bring your right foot alongside your left. Now try to lift your head from the wall.

Impossible, but why? Your friends are leaning too far forward to pull their heads away from the wall.

49

Heavy Leg

Stand with your hand out in front of you at knee level and bring one knee up to touch it. Ask a friend to do the same—while standing next to a wall.

To set up this trick, make sure your friend stands with *left shoulder* and *foot* up against a wall. Then hold your hand in front of his or her *right* knee and say, "Try to touch my hand with your knee and keep it there for a couple of seconds." This movement is impossible, because to raise one foot more than a little way off the ground means a person must shift his or her weight far to the left and the wall is in the way.

Floating Finger

You can make a "sausage" appear and float in mid-air between your friends' two index fingers.

1. Tell your friends to put the tips of their index fingers together about 12cm/5 inches in front of their eyes. They should focus on some distance beyond, not on their finger tips.

2. When they move their fingers slowly apart they will see a "sausage" floating through the air.

If they don't see a "sausage" the first time, they should move their fingers closer or farther away from their eyes until they do.

How does this work? Because our right eye sees our index fingers from a different angle than our left eye does, our brain receives overlapping images of the finger tips. It's these overlapping images that form the "sausage."

See-through Hand

You can make a hole appear in the palm of a friend's hand.

Tell a friend to roll up a sheet of paper into a tube about 2.5 cm/1 inch in diameter, then give him or her these instructions.

1. Keep both eyes open and hold the tube to your right eye like a telescope.

2. Hold your other hand flat with fingers together and palm toward you. Place it alongside the far end of the tube so that the edge of your hand touches the tube.

3. Slide your hand slowly up the tube toward your face until a hole appears.

The hole appears because the brain doesn't like getting different images from each eye. So it joins the images together and you "see" through your hand what your left eye should be seeing.

Magnetic Fingers

**Announce that you can mag-
netize people's fingers so
that they won't be able to
separate them.**

Demonstrate how this trick
works by placing your knuckles together and pressing
your index fingers together.
Keep your elbows well apart.
Separate your index fingers.
Do the same with your second

fingers, and have the audience
do it with you. Next, cast a
spell over your audience. Then
ask them to put their third
fingers together then try with
all their might to separate
them.

Impossible. But why? The
muscles of your third finger
are weaker than the others—
much too weak to push
against the muscles keeping
your knuckles together.

Whatsit?

If you pass behind this pole, you shrink? Find out what's really happening on page 95.

Jungle Jokes

Q. What time is it when a hippopotamus sits on a chair?
A. Time to get a new chair.

Q. Where do you find hippos?
A. It all depends on where you put them.

Q. What's as big as a hippopotamus and weighs nothing?
A. A hippopotamus's shadow.

Q. Why do ostriches have such long legs?

A. So their feet will touch the ground.

Q. What's worse than a giraffe with a sore throat?

A. A hippo with chapped lips.

Q. What do you get when you cross a canary with a tiger?

A. We don't know, but if it sings, you'd better listen.

Q. Where does a fully grown gorilla sleep?

A. Anywhere it wants to.

Q. What do monkeys eat for dessert?

A. Chocolate chimp cookies.

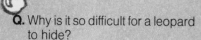

Q. Why is it so difficult for a leopard to hide?

A. Because it's always spotted.

Q. What animal can jump higher than a house?

A. All of them. A house can't jump.

Q. Why should an elephant carry a key?

A. To unlock its trunk.

Q. What's gray and stomps out forest fires?

A. Smokey the Elephant.

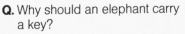

Q. What did the elephant do when it broke its toe?

A. It called a toe truck.

Q. How can you tell if there's an elephant in your refrigerator?

A. By the footprints in the butter.

Q. When an elephant comes to visit, how do you know it is going to stay?

A. It brings its trunk.

Q. Why did the elephant sit on the marshmallow?

A. To keep from falling in the cocoa.

Q. Why do elephants have sore ankles?

A. They wear their sneakers too tight.

Q. How do you keep an elephant from going through the eye of a needle?

A. Tie a knot in its tail.

61

Whatsit?

When you stop scratching your brow, you can read about these four heads on page 95.

Q. Where would a tiger go if it lost its tail?

A. To the re-tail store.

Q. What do you call it when giraffes moving one way get mixed up with giraffes moving another way?

A. A giraffic jam.

Q. If you were surrounded by 30 lions, 25 elephants and 10 hippos, how would you get away from them?

A. Step off the merry-go-round.

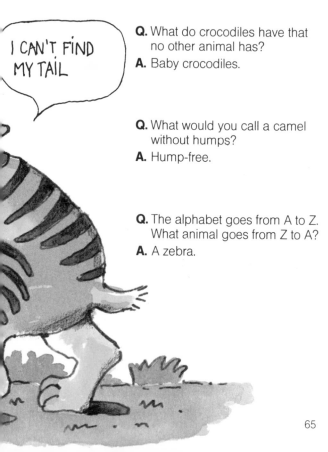

Q. What do crocodiles have that no other animal has?

A. Baby crocodiles.

Q. What would you call a camel without humps?

A. Hump-free.

Q. The alphabet goes from A to Z. What animal goes from Z to A?

A. A zebra.

Funny Name Game

Leaping leopards! Did you know that some groups of animals have very silly names? For instance, a group of leopards is called a leap.

Can you tell by looking at the illustrations of these animals what the name of their group is?

We're a _____ of toads.

We're a

_____

of gorillas.

We're a

_____

of plovers.

We're a

_____

of hounds.

We're a

_____

of moles.

Answers on page 95

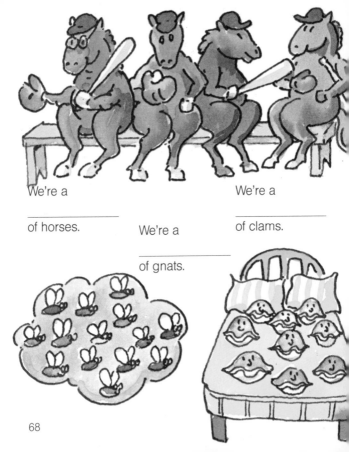

We're a

_____

of horses.

We're a

_____

of gnats.

We're a

_____

of clams.

We're a

_____

of fish.

We're a

_____

of goats.

Whatsit?

How can they play when they won't face the net?
For the real score, turn to page 95.

Group Gags

Q. What do moose do at a concert?
A. Make moosic.

Q. What keys are too big to carry in your pocket?
A. Donkeys, turkeys and monkeys.

Q. Why did the chickens run across the tennis court?
A. Because the referee called fowl.

Q. What has 18 legs, red spots and catches flies?
A. A baseball team with measles.

Q. What kind of dots dance?
A. Polka dots.

Q. Where do moths like to dance?
A. At a moth ball.

73

Q. Why do you have to be careful when it's raining dogs and cats?

A. You might step in a poodle.

Q. What would you have if all the cars in the nation were pink?

A. A pink car-nation.

Q. If two is company, and three's a crowd, what are four and five?

A. Nine.

74

Q. How would you start a firefly race?

A. On your mark, get set, glow.

Q. Why do monsters make good football players?

A. Because they always reach the ghoul-line.

YIPE!!

Q. What kind of ears do mountains have?

A. Mountaineers.

75

Animal Foolers

Meet some animal masters of disguise. Their disguises may look funny to us, but these animals can fool even the hungriest predator into not eating them.

If you said that this was a picture of two twigs, look again. The twig on the right is real, but the twig on the left is a caterpillar called a looper.

What pretty flowers—or are they? What may look like lovely white blossoms are really clusters of East African larval plant hoppers.

If you want to hide in a jungle, you might take a tip from the tropical katydid. This insect disguises itself with wings that look like leaves.

77

Any insect foolhardy enough to come near what looks like this half-eaten leaf is in for a nasty surprise. That's because that "leaf" is the dangerous devil mantis.

This confusing mess of spines and bumps is really a scorpion fish. Enemies are so bewildered when they see it that they usually swim past.

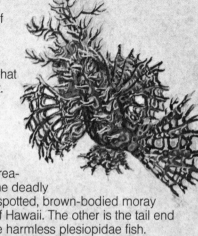

One of these creatures is the deadly white spotted, brown-bodied moray eel of Hawaii. The other is the tail end of the harmless plesiopidae fish. Most enemies don't stay around long enough to find out who they are meeting.

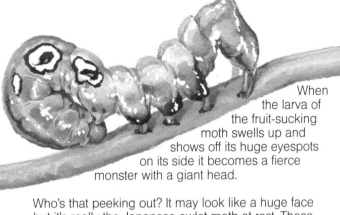

When the larva of the fruit-sucking moth swells up and shows off its huge eyespots on its side it becomes a fierce monster with a giant head.

Who's that peeking out? It may look like a huge face but it's really the Japanese owlet moth at rest. Those "eyes" are markings on its wings to scare away enemies.

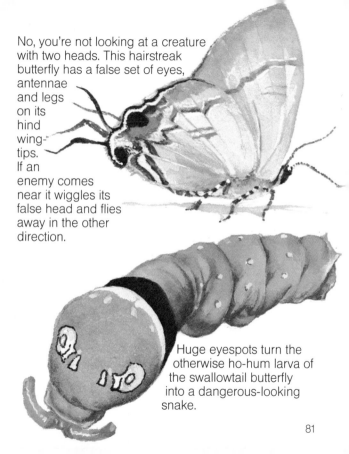

No, you're not looking at a creature with two heads. This hairstreak butterfly has a false set of eyes, antennae and legs on its hind wing-tips. If an enemy comes near it wiggles its false head and flies away in the other direction.

Huge eyespots turn the otherwise ho-hum larva of the swallowtail butterfly into a dangerous-looking snake.

81

When this mild-mannered balloon fish wants to scare off enemies, it gulps down lots of air and puffs itself into a big prickly ball.

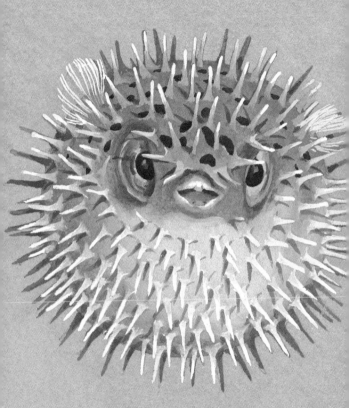

What Am I?

Answers on page 95

These riddles are about things that you see or hear about almost every day. But the way these things are presented here means you must think about them in a new way.

1. I have four legs and a tail and eat hay. I see just as well from either end. I'm _____.

2. I happen once in every minute, but twice in every moment. But I never happen at all in a hundred thousand years. I'm _____.

3. The more you take away from me, the bigger I become. I'm _____.

4. I'm sometimes green and sometimes brown. I'm usually taller than you but sometimes I can be the size of a pencil eraser. I'm _____.

5. I fly high in the sky, but I'm not a kite. I hold lots of water, but I'm not a pond. I'm _____.

6. I have a mouth but I never talk. I have a bed but I never sleep. I'm _____.

85

Funny Fliers

Q. Why do birds fly south for winter?

A. Because it's too far to walk.

Q. What do you call a seagull that flies over the bay?

A. A bagel.

Q. What happens when an owl gets laryngitis?

A. It doesn't give a hoot.

Q. What bird is present at every meal?

A. The swallow.

Q. What do birds say on Halloween?

A. Trick or tweet.

Q. Why does a stork stand on one leg?

A. So it won't fall over.

Q. What do you get when you cross a bee with a doorbell?

A. A hum-dinger.

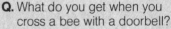
SOUTH

Astro Nuts

Q. What kind of sandwiches do astronauts eat?
A. Launchmeat sandwiches.

Q. What do Martians who use the metric system say?
A. Take me to your liter.

Q. If athletes get athlete's foot, what do astronauts get?
A. Missile toe.

SPLAT

Q. What did the astronaut see on the stove?

A. An unidentified frying object.

Q. When is it hard to get a ticket to the moon?

A. When it's full.

Q. How do you get to an ice cream parlor in outer space?

A. Take the Milky Way.

Spooky Stuff

Q. What do witches put on their hair?

A. Scare-spray.

Q. Why do witches ride brooms?

A. Because vacuum cleaners are too heavy.

Q. What holds the moon up?

A. Moon beams.

Q. What stars did the sheriff put in jail?

A. Shooting stars.

Q. What do ghosts put on their feet?

A. Ghoul-oshes.

Q. Why do vampires brush their teeth?

A. To stop bat breath.

Whatsit?

Why is this fur flying? Find out on page 95.

Answers

Whatsit? Pages 6-7

The goose in the middle is *not* taking a clumsy nose dive into the water. What you see is a still-water reflection of the very graceful goose above.

Whatsit? Pages 16-17

It's not every day you see a hen in a pond. But this hen has adopted these ducklings as her own and where they go, she follows.

Whatsit? Pages 22-23

A rooster playing soccer is an odd sight in any farmyard. This sporting rooster belongs to the Dean family of Camarillo, California, U.S.A., and can kick the ball a distance of 4 m/12 feet. Any soccer player —feathered or not—would be proud of that feat.

Whatsit? Pages 32-33

When Annette Wasko of Los Molinas, California, U.S.A., was nine years old, she had a pet called Dandelion who *loved* to pull her around in a cart. Of course, they baa-fulled everyone.

Whatsit? Pages 40-41

Meet the Walking Machine invented by the employees of Honda in Japan as part of the company's 7th Idea Contest. How many feet do you think it can travel per minute?

Whatsit? Page 45

Constable John Powers of Waterloo, Ontario, Canada, could cause a few traffic jams. Happily, he only shows off his "flying jewels" when he gives scientific talks on butterflies to community groups.

Whatsit? Pages 54-55

What you see is the back end of an adult bighorned sheep and the front end of a 12-day-old bighorn.

Whatsit? Pages 62-63

Of course, there are four giraffes. What a wonderful photograph!

Funny Name Game

Pages 66-69

A *knot*
A *band*
A *congregation*
A *cry*
A *labor*
A *team*
A *cloud*
A *bed*
A *trip*
A *school*

Whatsit? Pages 70-71

These geese have been herded onto a tennis court by officials at Stanley Park in Vancouver, British Columbia, Canada. They're waiting to be transported to other parks that don't have so many geese.

What Am I? Pages 84-85

1. a horse, with its eyes shut, of course
2. the letter "m"
3. a hole
4. a corn plant
5. a cloud
6. a river

Whatsit? Pages 92-93

This high-flying "Putty Cat" loves nothing better than hanging around with its owner, Patty Butler of Salinas, California, U.S.A.

Photo Credits:
pp
6-7 Vancouver Province, Rick Loughran
16-17 Canadian Press
22-23 Canadian Press
32-33 U.P.I.
40-41 Canadian Press
45 Constable John Powers
54-55 Winnipeg Free Press
62-63 Canadian Press
70-71 Vancouver Sun
92-93 Canadian Press
Illustrations:
47-53 Tony Thomas
76-83 Olena Kassian